639.9   Pringle, Laurence P.
PRI   Saving our wildlife.

                        33197000019401

$15.95

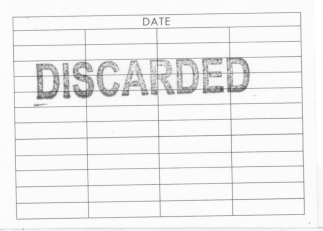

Saving Our Wildlife

Laurence Pringle

ENSLOW PUBLISHERS, INC.

Bloy St. & Ramsey Ave.
Box 777
Hillside, N.J. 07205
U.S.A.

P.O. Box 38
Aldershot
Hants GU12 6BP
U.K.

Library of Congress Cataloging–in–Publication Data

Pringle, Laurence P.
  Saving our wildlife / by Laurence Pringle.
    p. cm.
  Bibliography: p.
  Includes index.
  Summary: Explains the importance of wildlife and the ways in which people are trying to save various species in North America.

  ISBN 0-89490-204-0

  1.Wildlife conservation—United States—Juvenile literature.
[1. Wildlife conservation.] I. Title.

QL84.2.P75   1990
639.9—dc20   89-32872
                                                CIP
                                                AC

Printed in the United States of America
10 9 8 7 6 5 4 3

Illustration Credits:
Colorado Dept. of Natural Resources, photo by Geoff Tischbein: 23, 55; Earthwatch: 6; Michigan Dept. of Natural Resources: 32; New York Historical Society, New York City: 10; New York State Dept. of Environmental Conservation (Bruce Penrod): 30; Laurence Pringle: 15, 19, 28, 38; Student Conservation Association: 60; U.S. Dept. of the Interior. Fish and Wildlife Service: 8, 13, 17, 25, 51, (Gary D. Zahm: 22; Jeff Foott: 35; Steve Maslowski: 43; Jessie Grantham: 49); Wisconsin Dept. of Natural Resources: 57; © 1987 Wyoming Game and Fish Dept. (LuRay Parker): 46, 47.

Contents

1   *A Place for Wildlife* 5

2   *Defending Habitats* 12

3   *Another Chance* 27

4   *Back to the Wild* 40

Saving Nongame Wildlife 54

Working to Save Wildlife 58

Further Reading 61

Index 63

*Dedicated to Oliver Hewitt and
W. J. Hamilton, Jr., who helped
me on my way.*

1

A Place for Wildlife

In New York State, plans for a shopping mall are changed so that a few acres of land remain as habitat for a rare butterfly. In California, biologists capture the last wild condors in a controversial step aimed at saving the birds from extinction. And in North Carolina, captive red wolves are trained so they will have a chance to survive when they are turned loose in the wild.

All over North America people are working to save wildlife. The efforts range from local centers that rescue injured birds, to national and international organizations that raise money to buy precious habitats. The participants include ecologists and other scientists, law enforcement agents who arrest poachers, and concerned citizens.

"Why?" is not a question these people ask about their activities. Their values and feelings lead them to help save wildlife, and also wild plants. They treasure a diversity of living things. They believe that a pond or forest with all or most of its natural variety of animals and plants is more interesting and esthetically pleasing than a ruined, impoverished habitat. Many of them also believe that wild animals have a right to exist on earth. These creatures are our fellow passengers on Spaceship Earth.

Holding a vulture, this Earthwatch volunteer worked on a bird study near Malheur Lake, Oregon.

Such views are not shared, however, by some politicians, business people, economists, and others. Does it really matter, they ask, if California condors or black-footed ferrets or manatees become extinct? We can get along fine without these and many other wild animals, they argue.

Confronted by these questions and attitudes, biologists respond in terms of economics, and even of human survival. All wild animals and plants are resources. Some we have a practical use for now; some we may need in the future.

Biologists have elaborated on these views before congressional committees. In 1982, Thomas Eisner of Cornell University, a biologist who specializes in the chemical compounds derived from animals and plants, told of an insect repellent found in millipedes and a potential heart drug in fireflies. He also reported that chemicals found in sea slugs have potential as cancer-fighting drugs. In all, many hundreds of wild animal species have already proved useful to humans, and we have hardly scratched the surface of the potential value of others, most of which we know little about. Since we don't know which species may prove invaluable, it seems wise to preserve as many as possible.

Each species has three basic requirements for survival. One is having enough of the physical habitat to which it is adapted. Even common kinds of wildlife have certain habitat needs, which may be more specific and subtle than we at first suspect. A widespread forest songbird, for example, may not be found in woods that lack the understory trees in which it nests. Some species require two distinct habitats to meet different needs. The red-winged and yellow-headed blackbirds of North America, for instance, nest in marshes but seek food on the ground elsewhere. Migratory birds may also have different habitat needs in different seasons. In the summer, some songbirds nest deep in North American forests; in winter, they live in more open, brushy habitats in Latin America.

Populations of common loons and black ducks have declined because acid rain has diminished the supply of aquatic insects on

7

which their young feed. The lakes and ponds where they nest may look the same as before, but a chemical change has altered their habitat for the worse. In contrast, populations of brown pelicans, ospreys, and eagles have rebounded because such pesticides as endrin and DDT (which sabotaged their reproduction) are no longer contaminating their habitats.

Raccoons and opossums are habitat "generalists" that can thrive in all sorts of places. Rare species, on the other hand, are habitat "specialists" that have very specific habitat needs. One example is the few hundred Kirtland's warblers that nest only under or near young jack pines in parts of six Michigan counties. The warblers are further

In many areas, populations of the osprey (fish hawk) have recovered since certain pesticides were banned.

limited because they do not occupy small stands of jack pines. They usually need at least 80 acres of habitat to establish a breeding population, and they reproduce best in stands of 200 acres or more.

This warbler illustrates another basic requirement for wildlife survival: having a large enough population so that the threat of extinction is slight. In the case of the Kirtland's warbler, extinction is a very real possibility. It has been prevented so far by land management steps—including deliberately set fires—that provide a habitat of young jack pines for warbler nest sites.

Small populations may suffer the effects of inbreeding between closely related mates. As a result, harmful genetic traits tend to increase and may cause the numbers to decline. Small populations are also vulnerable to catastrophes. In the case of the Kirtland's warblers, a hurricane striking their wintering grounds in the Bahamas could devastate the species.

A natural disaster—fire—was instrumental in wiping out the heath hen. People in Massachusetts were once hopeful about the survival chances of this bird—a species of prairie chicken that had been common in the Northeast but which was nearly wiped out in the 1800s by hunting and habitat destruction. As a result, by 1890 fewer than 100 of these birds survived on Martha's Vineyard, an island off the coast of Massachusetts. A refuge was established on the island, however, and by early 1916 the species had rebounded to as many as 2,000 individuals. Some birds were shipped to mainland Massachusetts and to Long Island, New York, in an unsuccessful attempt to reestablish populations that had died out.

Disaster struck in May of 1916, as a great fire swept through the heath hen reserve while the female birds were on their nests. About 100 birds survived, and the species had a partial revival, to about 400 individuals in 1921. But disease from poultry farms and predation from feral cats and dogs took their toll. In the springs of 1930, 1931, and 1932, an ornithologist saw a lone male heath hen perform its mating dance. No female responded. That male died and with it the species. Had populations existed in several places, the heath hen might have withstood the calamity that occurred at one site.

There is no specific "threshold" of population size that protects wildlife from harmful inbreeding or from other threats to survival. It varies from one species to another. There is no doubt, however, that this factor worries those who are trying to save populations of rare species.

Each wild animal is part of an entire animal-plant community. It is ecologically linked to other organisms, and its very survival depends on some of these links. This is the third basic factor in a species' survival—having enough of the other organisms that help sustain its life. Some insects and flowering plants, for example, have a "lock and

Reduced to living in one small part of its former range, the heath hen was highly vulnerable to extinction.

key" relationship, with just one kind of insect adapted to pollinate the plant's blossoms. Neither plant nor animal is likely to survive without the other.

In Florida, the rare snail kite, a species of hawk, feeds almost exclusively on freshwater snails, called apple snails. Destruction of freshwater ponds and marshes has reduced their population because it robs the kites of their food supply. They survive in the Everglades, but their numbers rise and fall with the annual rainfall. Rainy years provide plenty of habitats for apple snails, and the kites thrive. Drought years have the opposite effect.

Every wildlife species has different needs that affect the strategies used to protect it. The following chapters describe the many ways in which people are trying to save the wild animals of North America.

2

Defending Habitats

In Pennsylvania, a mountaintop that was once a favorite site for shooting migrating hawks is now visited by many thousands of people who come to watch hawks and eagles fly by. All over North America, wildlife that was once shot or trapped year round is now protected for at least part of each year by state or federal laws, or both. Public attitudes have also changed. The "hook and bullet press," as hunting and fishing magazines are called, seldom run articles about "vermin" and "varmits"—terms that were once applied to such animals as foxes and crows.

The days of wanton killing are over. Historically, it was primarily overhunting that led to the establishment of the first federal wildlife refuges in the United States. The refuge system began because all wildlife, including such game birds as ducks and other migratory waterfowl, were being slaughtered. President Theodore Roosevelt, a hunter himself, realized that waterfowl needed safe places along their migration routes. By 1904, at the end of Roosevelt's first term, 51 refuges had been set aside in the United States and its territories. Many were primarily waterfowl habitats, but some were saved for the benefit of such nongame birds as pelicans and spoonbills. Today there are more than 440 federal wildlife refuges totaling 92 million acres. Most of the acreage is in Alaska, but refuges are located all over the United States and its territories. In Canada, many wildlife species are protected in national and provincial parks, and in a system of 45 national wildlife areas and 99 migratory bird sanctuaries.

In addition, several dozen national parks, forests, and monuments, thousands of state and county parks and reserves, and numerous privately owned preserves provide habitat for wildlife in the United States. Many millions of acres have been set aside for protection of wild animals and plants. In the opinion of real estate developers, mining companies, and other business interests, this is plenty—perhaps too much.

Overhunting of ducks and geese led to the establishment of the federal wildlife refuge system of the United States.

On the other hand, environmental groups, ecologists, and many citizens believe that more habitats must be set aside. The result is a political struggle in state legislatures and in the United States Congress. Sometimes years of public education and political lobbying result in the establishment of a new reserve. (It is often smaller than considered ideal by those seeking to maintain a diversity of habitats and living things). In the late 1980s, for example, efforts continued to establish a Tall Grass Prairie National Preserve in Oklahoma and to expand the Death Valley and Joshua Tree monuments of California into full national parks. The opponents of the latter proposals include organized groups of off-road-vehicle riders.

A Growing Interest in Nongame Animals

Establishing a wildlife reserve does not end controversy. Hunting, trapping, and fishing are allowed in national forests, many federal wildlife refuges, and also in numerous state parks. These activities are regulated and do not normally reduce wildlife populations. But some people believe there has been an overemphasis on improving conditions for game animals on the state level and in national wildlife refuges. For example, land may be cleared to provide food for ducks and geese, to the detriment of songbirds, amphibians, and other kinds of animals that are not hunted. In 1987, legislation was introduced in Congress that aimed to prohibit hunting and trapping on national wildlife refuges.

Enlightened hunters and fishermen were pioneers in efforts to save wildlife. Today such groups as Trout Unlimited, the Izaak Walton League, and the National Wildlife Federation continue to be concerned about wildlife that is hunted or fished for by people, but seek to help nongame animals too. They now recognize that saving habitat is the key to saving all wildlife and that the survival of game animals is linked to that of many nongame organisms. Similarly, the National Audubon Society, which began as a bird conservation group, today tackles a broad range of environmental problems.

14

Ninety percent or more of all wild animals in North America are nongame species. Studies at federal wildlife refuges have shown that, for every hunter who enters, more than two dozen other people go to watch birds, hike, take nature photographs, and the like. The same is true of many state wildlife areas.

Historically, however, programs aimed at nongame animals have received 20 percent or less of the wildlife funds spent by federal and state wildlife agencies. This allocation is understandable, since funds for these programs have come largely from sales of hunting and fishing licenses and from federal excise taxes on equipment used by hunters and fishermen.

Nongame species, including whitefooted mice, are now receiving more attention from state natural resource agencies.

This emphasis began to shift in the early 1970s, when such states as New York and California began projects aimed at saving populations of rare nongame wildlife. Growing concern about endangered species increased interest in such projects in other states. In 1977 the state of Colorado gave each taxpayer an opportunity, on his or her income-tax form, to give a few dollars to support programs aimed at aiding nongame wildlife. Similar tax checkoffs for nongame (and for endangered plants, too, in some states) have since been established in thirty-three other states. In 1985 these state tax checkoffs produced $9 million.

In some states, these "gifts to wildlife" funds have declined because taxpayers have been offered checkoffs for other worthy causes. The amount of money may also vary from year to year, making long-range planning difficult. Nevertheless, these funds make possible a broad range of studies, habitat purchases, and other steps toward saving nongame wildlife.

Nongame wildlife has long been a concern for many private organizations that help establish nature preserves in North America. Some are national in scope, some work in just one region or state, and some spring up to save a single wild area. In western Connecticut, for example, a group of citizens began in the 1950s to buy parts of a deep, narrow, forested river valley. About 350 acres along two and a half miles of the valley are now owned by the Mianus River Gorge Conservation Committee.

In contrast, the Nature Conservancy is a national group that is responsible for preserving more than three million acres of forests, marshes, prairies, mountains, deserts, and islands. Its projects range in size from less than an acre to 220,000 acres. The Nature Conservancy actually owns and oversees about 60 percent of the sites it has protected. The rest have become the responsibility of state or federal natural resource agencies.

The conservancy frequently plays a vital role in rescuing a wild area from development by buying it, then later being reimbursed by a government agency that takes title to the land. In 1984 the Nature Conservancy helped save a unique wild area in southern Nevada. Ash Meadows is a spring-fed wetland "island" in a sea of desert. It harbors more than two dozen animals and plants found nowhere else in the world. Several, including the Devil's Hole pupfish, are ranked as endangered or threatened species.

Part of this area was drained in the 1960s, and more was threatened by use of wells that were drilled by an agricultural company to provide irrigation water. The water level in the 43-acre Devil's Hole dropped. The National Park Service sued the agricultural company in order to protect the endangered pupfish, and in 1976 the United States Supreme Court limited the use of ground water for agricultural purposes.

The battle to save the wild animals and plants of Ash Meadows was far from over, however. The agricultural company sold its acreage to resort developers, who planned golf courses, manmade lakes,

The Nature Conservancy played a vital role in preserving much of Nevada's desert oasis area called Ash Meadows.

casinos, and thousands of homes. They began to build roads and divert the outflow of natural pools. Then the threat of lawsuits by environmental groups slowed development. The Nature Conservancy became actively involved in the early 1980s and, after long and complex negotiations with the developers, bought 12,613 acres at Ash Meadows. The conservancy then sold the wetlands to the Fish and Wildlife Service. In 1984, this acreage, added to land already owned by the federal government, became the Ash Meadows National Wildlife Refuge.

Threatened Islands of Wildness

Wildlife cannot exist without its habitat, but saving that habitat does not ensure survival of wildlife. Key animals and plants may be threatened and lost as a result of natural forces, management choices, or factors beyond a refuge's borders.

The Kirtland's warbler, for example, would die out if all of its jack pine habitat was left alone and grew into a mature pine forest. Instead, fires are set to keep large tracts of land in the early stage of forest succession needed by this species. Controlled burning is required to provide habitat for other rare species, including the Karner blue butterflies in New York's Pine Bush region (near Albany) and in virtually all prairie preserves. Fire was a vital natural force in prairie ecosystems; it must be allowed and often deliberately started after careful planning for prairie reserves to thrive.

Letting nature take its course can be disastrous, especially on small reserves. A number of refuges have an overabundance of deer. In Ipswich, Massachusetts, the 2,100-acre Crane Reservation and Wildlife Refuge had in 1985 a deer population estimated to be four times greater than its vegetation could support. Some deer starved to death each winter. Trees were stripped of twigs and leaves as high as deer could reach. Furthermore, the natural vegetation of the area was altered—the deer had eliminated several kinds of wildflowers, while honeysuckle, which they do not eat, dominated the undergrowth.

18

Wolves and other natural predators of deer cannot survive on such a small area, especially one with half a million annual visitors. So, in 1985 the trustees of this private refuge proposed a solution: reduce the deer population by limited hunting. Animal rights activists opposed this step, but eventually two animal rights groups agreed that deer were starving and that the controlled hunt was more humane. In three years the deer population was cut by about two-thirds, and the reserve's plant life began to recover.

Much larger natural areas may also face problems of overabundant large grazing animals. Rocky Mountain National Park in Colorado, for example, totals nearly 267,000 acres. Elk, a native species, have increased to a population of about 4,000. Their overgrazing damages aspen forests that are the habitat of other species.

The park's management has recommended that wolves be released as a way to keep the elk herd in check, but many nearby ranchers oppose the idea. The elk may eventually be reduced by factors

Lacking their natural predators, deer and other large grazing mammals may become so abundant that they devastate their favorite food plants. Some die of starvation.

beyond the park's borders. They normally migrate to lower elevations outside the park in winter, but their winter range is shrinking as housing subdivisions cover the land.

This development is particularly troublesome because elk have always ranged beyond the park's borders. So, for some species, the habitat adjacent to a park or other reserve may be as vital as the habitat within.

A refuge set aside for wildlife can become a sort of island that is too small for the long-term survival of some kinds of wildlife. For more than two decades, ecologists have studied forests, mountaintops, and other land habitats as though they were islands surrounded by water. There are similarities: like an island in the sea, a forest may be so isolated from other woods that insects, mammals, and other organisms cannot recolonize it and revive populations that have died out. Ecologists who studied forest islands in Wisconsin found fewer species and smaller populations of wild mammals in suburban areas. The reason, they concluded, was "greater isolation of islands and the absence of diverse adjacent habitat" in suburbia.

Ecologists who studied bird populations also concluded that large tracts of forest—of hundreds or even thousands of acres—are needed so that regular recolonization can occur. They referred to small birds; large mammals need even more space. A study published in 1987 revealed that national parks as vast as Yosemite (833 square miles) and Mount Rainier (390 square miles) have lost some of the large mammal species that existed when the parks were established more than eighty years ago.

"When I got into this business," said ecologist Dr. Jared Diamond of the University of California at Los Angeles, "I had the naive hope that a lot of biologists shared, that what you need to do is set up a national park and keep your hands off it—nature will take care of itself. That's fine if you've got a perfectly gigantic national park, but when you set up a small national park, you cut off all kinds of natural processes."

We now know that it is vital to make wildlife reserves as large as possible—and to add to their acreage whenever possible. When only small reserves can be saved, corridors of natural habitat between them keep these "islands" from becoming totally isolated.

In 1986 the President's Commission on Americans Outdoors recommended such corridors, either on land or along waterways, to link natural areas so that "wildlife would not be isolated in small green islands in a widening sea of urban civilization."

The Most Troublesome Species, *Homo sapiens*

More active management is needed and has been implemented at some national parks. One step is to get rid of alien species (such as burros and feral pigs) that compete with native species. It is increasingly obvious, however, that human activities beyond the borders of wildlife reserves threaten the well-being and even the survival of the wildlife within. Water use by farmers may reduce the normal flow of water that sustains wildlife within a reserve. This problem occurs at Everglades National Park in Florida and at several wildlife refuges in the arid West, including the Stillwater Wildlife Management Area in Nevada.

Sometimes the problem is not the quantity of water but its quality. A 1985 survey of all federal wildlife refuges revealed that more than a quarter had polluted waters. Most of the contamination came from agricultural lands. Rainwater running off the land carried fertilizers, pesticides, and herbicides. Several refuges had outbreaks of diseases that killed large numbers of birds.

By far the worst case was at Kesterson National Wildlife Refuge near Palo Alto in California's San Joaquin Valley. In 1981, runoff from irrigated agricultural land was allowed to drain into a large reservoir that is part of the refuge. The water contained not just agricultural chemicals but also large amounts of salt and selenium, an element abundant in the valley's soils. Excess selenium has been known to cause cancers and birth defects in animals. Water draining into the reservoir also contained high levels of arsenic, boron, cadmium, and copper.

The Kesterson reservoir changed from a refuge to a death trap. By 1982, nearly all bass, catfish, and other fish were gone. In 1983 the Fish and Wildlife Service began finding many dead birds, including newborn ducks, grebes, and stilts that lacked wings or eyes. The state water board intervened on grounds that the reservoir was an unregulated toxic dump. It was drained and is being filled in to reduce the hazard of contact by people and wildlife with selenium-tainted water or soils. During the process of filling the former reservoir with soil, ponds sometimes formed, and the Fish and Wildlife Service had the

An American avocet at Kesterson reservoir, where selenium-tainted water harmed birds that sought refuge there.

unusual job of scaring birds away to other parts of the refuge. Precautions are now taken to keep selenium-tainted drainwater from reaching other ponds and marshes of the refuge.

Managing people, including visitors and nearby residents, is a major challenge to those who administer parks and other wildlife refuges. Visitors to national parks hit a record 287 million in 1987 and are projected to grow to 450 million over the next two decades. At Rocky Mountain National Park, biologists are concerned about the human impact on bighorn sheep. One protective step is to close a hiking trail near their main habitat during the early summer lambing season. Visitors are also warned that the sheep are especially sensitive

Bighorn sheep must be protected from close contact with the growing numbers of visitors to Rocky Mountain Park.

to human intrusion; contact with people seems to increase their death rate from diseases.

One day park superintendent James Thompson saw a tourist park his car and scramble up a hillside with a camera, heading toward some bighorn sheep. " 'I told him sheep can die when stressed by human activity.' And he said, 'I don't care, as long as I get my picture.' "

Numerous state and federal laws protect wildlife, including endangered species, but there is still a large business in the meat, skins, and other parts of illegally killed wild animals. Law enforcement agents often use undercover operations to catch the wildlife killers. They sometimes set up "stings," posing as buyers of illegal game and fish. In 1985, after a two-year investigation, federal and state agents arrested 135 people in several northeastern states. Deer and waterfowl had been killed illegally for meat; eagles, ospreys, owls, and other birds for their plumage or for mounting as trophies.

Arrests have also been made near large national parks in the West, where the targeted species both outside and within the parks were golden eagles, mountain goats, and bears. A black bear's teeth, toenails, skin, and gallbladder may be worth several hundred dollars. Teeth and toenails are used in necklaces. Gallbladders are dried and sold in the Orient, where they are believed to have medicinal value. In 1989, ten people in the eastern United States were arrested for killing more than 400 black bears for their gallbladders and other marketable parts.

Sad to say, the rarer the species, the more valuable its dead carcass on the black market. Parts of a grizzly bear—an endangered species— are worth as much as $15,000. Since 1983, the National Audubon Society has offered a $10,000 reward for information leading to the arrest of grizzly bear poachers. It has been paid several times, with the convicted bear killers receiving stiff sentences.

The United States is one of ninety-five nations that has signed a treaty and joined a group aimed at stopping illegal trade in rare animals and plants. Begun in 1973, the Convention on International Trade in

This illegally taken wildlife, mostly from Alaska, includes a grizzly bear rug, snowy owl, and mountain goats.

Endangered Species of Wild Flora and Fauna (known as CITES) meets annually. Regrettably, a nation's CITES membership does not ensure an end to its participation in the deadly commerce of rare living forms. Japan, for instance, has allowed itself exemptions for such animal parts as monitor lizard skins and crocodile hides because it has domestic industries that depend on these imports. In other nations, corrupt officials and lax enforcement of protective laws allow a thriving wildlife trade to continue. It is estimated as a $5 billion a year business.

The CITES treaty is only as good as its enforcement, and that has improved. Trade in the skins of cheetahs, leopards, and other spotted cats has been curbed. Strong political pressure from CITES members has caused some wildlife-importing countries to take steps against illegal trade.

The United States has more enforcement tools than many other countries. As a wealthy nation, however, it represents a big market for imported animals, plants, and their parts. Some people in the United States are willing to pay many thousands of dollars for "something the other guy doesn't have," whether it is a rare live orchid or parrot, the skin of an endangered reptile, or an ivory tusk from one of the dwindling numbers of African elephants. Without collectors willing to buy, this smuggling would end.

Along with other developed countries, the United States has a special responsibility to see that its citizens do not "collect" some unique wild species to extinction.

3

Another Chance

Had a list of endangered species been compiled early in this century, it would have included bison, beavers, wild turkeys, egrets, wood ducks, pronghorns, Rocky Mountain elk, and trumpeter swans. In 1910, most authorities considered sea otters to be already extinct.

All of these species are with us today. With the exception of California sea otters and trumpeter swans, they are not threatened with extinction, and some occupy large parts of their former range. These species were saved from extinction mainly by laws that protected them from wanton slaughter, and also by protection of their habitats. Wildlife biologists also gave many once-scarce species a boost by releasing individuals in places where populations had been wiped out. These "reintroductions," as they are called, continue to be a vital part of the effort to save wild life.

Most of the early projects involved species that were valued by hunters, trappers, or fishermen, who supported the efforts of state wildlife departments to bring back ducks, beavers, and Atlantic salmon. Among many success stories, the comeback of wild turkeys is outstanding. Five subspecies live in the United States. In 1930, the total population was estimated at just 20,000 birds that survived in

Given a chance, bison came back from the brink of extinction.

scattered pockets in twenty-one states. Today, wild turkeys number 2 million and live in every state except Alaska. (They can be found now in several states where there is no record of previous occurrence.)

This success didn't come easily. It involved years of trial and error by wildlife biologists and was delayed by political obstacles. In their first attempts to replenish stocks of wild turkeys and to restore them to suitable habitats, game managers crossbred wild and domestic turkeys. They hoped to mass-produce wild turkeys on game farms. They succeeded in raising plenty of turkeys this way, but the product was not a true wild turkey. Two months after release, some of these birds still allowed people to approach to within a few feet before showing alarm and were not capable of surviving long in the wild.

This fact was noted as early as 1944, but many state game departments persisted in turning out game farm turkeys—cannon fodder for hunters. Over a span of more than two decades, wildlife biologists also used game farm turkeys in attempts to reestablish populations. Of 354 reintroduction attempts in twenty-three states, 331 were failures.

In 1959, New York abandoned turkey farming and began a program of trapping live wild turkeys and releasing them in favorable habitats. Catching turkeys is difficult, so progress was slow, but there *was* progress: the transplanted birds usually survived and established thriving populations. Many other state game departments launched similar programs. Biologists developed a device called the cannon net that enabled them to catch several wild turkeys at a time.

In many states, biologists tried to help newly released wild turkeys through the winter by setting up feeding stations. This practice actually reduced the birds' chances of long-term survival by concentrating them in small areas and not allowing natural forces to weed out the less fit birds. Once winter feeding was abandoned, the success rate of wild turkey reintroductions soared.

Similar trap-and-release programs have helped reestablish many other wildlife species. In the 1930s, beavers lived only in parts of the

29

Rocky Mountains, northern Maine, and the wilder parts of several Great Lakes states. Today they thrive in all states of their original range. In 1935 the trumpeter swan was in worse straits than the beaver: less than 100 survived south of Canada. Their habitat was protected by the establishment of the Red Rock Lakes Migratory Bird Refuge in Montana. The swans' growing numbers—from 97 in 1935 to 642 in 1954—enabled biologists to transfer some birds and successfully recolonize other federal refuges and Yellowstone National Park.

The reintroduction process continues. Missouri, Wisconsin, Michigan, and Ontario, Canada, are trying to reestablish trumpeter swans. They were killed off in Michigan in the 1880s. A restoration

The comeback of the wild turkey began when biologists started to reintroduce truly wild birds into new habitats.

program aims to have two separate breeding flocks by the year 2000. The first attempt, in 1986, failed because snapping turtles killed four young swans soon after they hatched. (The trumpeter swan eggs, mostly obtained from zoos, were incubated by mute swans, a related but nonnative species. This method of using another species as foster parents is called cross-fostering.)

Biologists killed hundreds of snapping turtles at the marsh where the reintroductions were tried. In 1987, four swans survived from 11 hatchlings, and in 1988 eight survived from 16 eggs that hatched. Adult trumpeter swans compete for food and space with mute swans, and some biologists feel strongly that the nonnative mute swans should be confined to zoos, leaving the natural habitat for native species. Once trumpeter swans are reestablished in Michigan, other states, and Ontario, steps may be taken to reduce or eliminate mute swans.

Each separate population of swans that is established lessens the chance that the entire species can be wiped out by a disease or other calamity. Whooping cranes were threatened by just such a disaster. In 1988, North America's best-known endangered species totaled about 150 wild birds and about 40 captive ones. (There were just 15 in the early 1940s.) For many years the whooping crane's only wintering grounds were in the Aransas National Wildlife Refuge in Texas. Teamwork by the United States Fish and Wildlife Service, the Canadian Wildlife Service, and the National Audubon Society has established one new population. These birds—just 16 in 1988—nest in the summer at Grays Lake National Wildlife Refuge in Idaho and spend winters at Bosque del Apache National Wildlife Refuge in New Mexico. By 1988 this project had cost $1.5 million, and the cranes were still not sustaining themselves by nesting successfully.

Biologists hope to establish a third whooping crane flock. The species' range originally extended from the Great Plains to the Atlantic. The cranes once nested in the freshwater marshes of Illinois, Minnesota, and other nearby states. Historical records reveal that they also lived in Florida. Sites under investigation for suitability as crane

As part of an effort in several states and in Canada to reestablish populations of trumpeter swans (above), Michigan biologists place eggs of trumpeter swans in a mute swan nest (below).

nesting habitat were located in central Florida and the Okefenokee Swamp of Georgia.

In the 1980s, wildlife reintroduction projects sometimes benefited from a growing interest in restoring prairies, forests, marshes, rivers, and other ecosystems. At hundreds of sites all over North America, ecologists are trying to restore damaged environments by ridding them of alien plants and animals and by encouraging native species. (At Nevada's Ash Meadows National Wildlife Refuge, for example, the Fish and Wildlife Service is restoring some drained and damaged wetlands.) Often some native species are missing, so their reintroduction is a vital step toward restoring a diverse plant-animal community.

At the world's largest prairie restoration project, on the lands of the Fermi National Accelerator Laboratory in Illinios, such native wildlife as coyotes, Savannah sparrows, and upland sand pipers have returned without human help. Ecologists expect that harriers and short-eared owls will also recolonize the restored prairie, but they plan to actively bring back Franklin's ground squirrels, prairie katydids, and other small creatures that once inhabited the Illinois prairie.

Welcome Back, Otter

Most wildlife reintroduction programs have broad public support. Hunters welcome the return of game species, and no one opposes aid for such rare and graceful birds as whooping cranes and trumpeter swans. For many years, however, the idea of reintroducing predatory animals was opposed by some. Hunters considered them competitors for wildlife they wanted for themselves. In the 1950s, for example, wildlife biologists in New York proposed that the fisher—a fox-sized member of the weasel family—be returned to its former range in the Catskill Mountains. The idea sparked protests from hunters and critical editorials about "turning killers loose."

By the mid-1970s, however, public understanding of the role of predators in nature had changed. Fishers were live-trapped in New York's Adirondack Mountains and let go in the Catskills, where they have thrived and spread. Fishers have also been successfully reintroduced to parts of the species' former range in Wisconsin, Montana, Idaho, Oregon, and other northern states.

Plans to reintroduce otters (also members of the weasel family) have also been opposed. Some fishermen mistakenly believe that river otters harm trout populations. On the West Coast, commercial abalone fishermen believe that sea otters eat too many of the shellfish they want to harvest and sell. To this day they oppose efforts to reintroduce sea otters to parts of their former range.

Sea otters once lived from Baja California up the North American coast and westward across the Aleutian Islands. Hunted for their fur, they were nearly wiped out by the beginning of this century. They began a slow comeback after being protected by an international treaty in 1911. Still, as few as fifty lived along the central California coast in 1936.

Both Canada and the United States have trapped and released sea otters in order to establish new populations along their coasts. The United States attempt began in 1987. The goal, similar to those for many other endangered species, was to start a new, separate population. Biologists feared that an oil spill or some other disaster might wipe out the one California colony in existence.

The 1989 *Exxon Valdez* oil spill in Prince William Sound, Alaska, killed several hundred sea otters in a few days and threatened others with eventual starvation. Before the accident, the Sound was home to about 15,000 sea otters.

From its low point in 1938, the California sea otter colony grew to about 1,650 sea otters spread along 200 miles of California coast. Of these otters, up to 70 a year for five years were to be moved to San Nicolas Island, 90 miles southwest of Los Angeles. The first 70 were captured by the summer of 1988. (The method: spot a sleeping otter floating on its back, race up to it in a boat, and catch it with a long-handled net.) They were flown to the waters off San Nicolas Island and released. The dream of quickly establishing a new sea otter colony was dashed, however, when some of the otters swam back to their former colony, 200 miles to the north. Others just disappeared. About 20 remained, and they seemed to be mostly young animals, so biologists planned to catch and release younger otters as the reintroduction went on.

Return of the Wolves

No wildlife reintroduction idea stirs up more opposition than bringing wolves back to habitats their ancestors once occupied. Although many people appreciate and even admire wolves, some are still stuck at the

Captured sea otters were flown to their new home near San Nicolas Island, west of Los Angeles.

"big bad wolf" nursery-rhyme level of knowledge about this endangered species.

Wolves were very nearly wiped out in the lower United States. In the early 1970s gray or timber wolves survived only in northern Minnesota and on Isle Royale National Park in Lake Superior. Wolves from Minnesota or Canada eventually recolonized parts of northern Michigan and Wisconsin; as of 1988, fewer than ten wolves lived in Michigan, and about twenty-five in Wisconsin. Much larger wolf populations exist in Alaska and Canada.

In 1975 the Fish and Wildlife Service began to study the chances of reestablishing wolves in other areas. There are numerous places in the United States where gray wolves might successfully be reintroduced. They include wilderness areas in Colorado, Oregon, Washington, northern California, and parts of the Southwest, as well as the Adirondack Mountains of New York.

The most promising sites, however, are located in the northern Rocky Mountains. No breeding population of the Rocky Mountain wolf, a subspecies of the timber wolf, was known to exist. A team of wolf experts devised the Northern Rocky Mountain Wolf Recovery Plan. It identified three areas that were big enough, wild enough, and in other ways good enough habitat for wolves. They are northwestern Montana (including the Glacier National Park-Bob Marshall Wilderness region), central Idaho (including the River of No Return and Selway-Bitterroot Wildernesses), and Yellowstone (including the national park, adjoining national forests, and other public lands).

Members of the wolf recovery team knew that any plan would spark opposition from the politically powerful western livestock industry, and they tried to devise a system for dealing with wolf predation on livestock, should it occur. Wolf recovery areas would be divided into three zones, with the least protection of wolves in zone three—those lands where wolves were most likely to encounter livestock, and where troublesome wolves could be caught and relocated, or killed if necessary.

Wolf experts do not expect much predation on livestock in the three proposed recovery areas. Their evidence comes from Alberta, Canada, and northern Minnesota—areas where wolves and livestock share the land. The state of Minnesota has a system for controlling wolves that kill livestock and for paying farmers for their losses. More than 1,000 wolves live in the vicinity of farms where 230,000 cattle and 90,000 sheep range. Nevertheless, during one study period, farmers never lost more than 7 cows, 98 calves, and 108 sheep in a year. In an average year, only about 40 of the 12,000 farms report or claim livestock losses from wolves. Many of these losses cannot be verified as wolf kills and may have been caused by coyotes or dogs. (In 1988 the environmental group called Defenders of Wildlife set up a $50,000 fund to compensate ranchers near Yellowstone National Park for verified livestock losses to wolves.)

Each of the three proposed recovery areas is much more remote than northern Minnesota. Each was chosen because of its wildness, its vast area of protected public lands, and the low numbers of nearby livestock. Nevertheless, western livestock ranchers opposed any deliberate reintroduction of wolves. Throughout most of the 1980s they used their political power in Congress to delay action on wolf recovery.

In the northernmost proposed recovery areas, it seems that wolves took matters into their own paws. Wolves were occasionally sighted in Glacier National Park during the 1970s. Then, in the early 1980s, biologists in both Alberta and Montana found increasing evidence that wolves were traveling south of the Canadian border. In 1985 a pack of twelve wolves moved into Glacier National Park. This was the first confirmed wolf pack residency in the western United States in fifty years.

The wolves have since reproduced. The initial pack divided, and some wolves returned to the Canadian side of the border. But other wolves have appeared east of Glacier National Park and in central Idaho. For reasons that biologists do not yet understand, wolves are now dispersing from Canada into favorable habitats in the western United States. Without any help from people, the Rocky Mountain wolf may recolonize two of the three wolf recovery sites.

The Yellowstone recovery area, with the national park as its center, lies several hundred miles from Canada and is unlikely to be colonized by Canadian wolves. Given enough time, it could be colonized by wolves from the Idaho or Glacier areas if wolf populations thrive there.

Wolf biologists and the general public would rather not wait. Every regional or national poll has shown strong support for bringing wolves back to the area. By a margin of six to one, visitors to Yellowstone believe that the presence of wolves would enrich their

There are several large wilderness areas in the western United States where wolves could be reestablished.

park experience. Sixty percent of those asked said that if wolves did not return by themselves, people should put them back. If carried out, this would be the first reintroduction of a predator to a national park.

Wolf experts consider Yellowstone *the* prime area for a new wolf population and see no reason for delay. It is the largest site, covering almost 3,500 square miles. The wolf's prey—elk, deer, bison, moose, pronghorn, beaver—are present in abundance. In the case of elk, it is overabundance: between 1968 and 1988, their population increased from 4,000 to 25,000.

"Yellowstone Park is a place that literally begs for wolves," said Dr. L. David Mech, who has studied them for more than thirty years in Minnesota and Canada. "It's teeming with prey; it used to have wolves; and all the species that were there originally should be restored. . . .To me, it's not a complete or natural wilderness to have all the species of prey that are there and not have the main predator they evolved with."

The executive director of the Wilderness Society, William Turnage, said of Yellowstone, "Of course the wolf belongs there. Someday we'll look back and wonder what all the fuss was about."

Wolves should thrive in Yellowstone. And the national park's two million annual visitors have no need to fear them. No healthy wild wolf has ever harmed a human in North America. Few people will even see the wary wolves. Greater numbers will have the extraordinary experience of hearing the wild music of their howls.

Ecologists strongly advocate reintroduction of wolves to Yellowstone. Success there would be good for wolves, for their prey, for the entire ecosystem, and for people. It would also give scientists an extraordinary opportunity to study the changes that occur as a major predator returns to fulfill its role in nature.

4

Back to the Wild

There are still plenty of good habitats in North America for mammoths and mastodons, yet they are extinct. Sometimes a species dies out or is close to extinction for reasons other than lack of habitat. Then we have a choice: to let it disappear or to give it a last chance in captivity, with some hope of later reestablishing the species in the wild. This approach is called captive breeding and today represents the only hope for several wild species of North America.

Captive breeding gets most of the credit for the return of the American bison. In the late nineteenth century there were many more bison in zoos and private, fenced-in game parks than in the wild. Bison from the New York Zoological Park (Bronx Zoo) were the nucleus of the herd that was established at the first bison refuge in Oklahoma. In modern times the Arabian oryx was rescued from near extinction by a captive breeding program. It has been successfully returned to the wild in Oman, Jordan, and Israel.

Three wildlife species at the brink of extinction in the United States have been given a reprieve in captivity. They are the red wolf, the California condor, and the black-footed ferret. The red wolf has already taken its first steps back to the wild.

The red wolf is somewhat smaller than the gray wolf. It hunts smaller prey and is less of a pack animal. It once ranged throughout the southeastern United States. Like other large predators, it was persecuted by generations of farmers and ranchers, not to mention employees of the Fish and Wildlife Service. Between 1955 and 1964 these trappers and poisoners killed 27,646 red wolves.

By the time this program stopped and the red wolf was declared an endangered species in 1967, only a few hundred survived in Louisiana and Texas. Given legal protection and living in adequate wild habitat, the red wolf was still faced with certain extinction. It was losing its genetic identity.

Under normal conditions, one species does not breed with another. But conditions for the red wolf were far from normal. In rapid decline, it increasingly came in contact with the coyote—a wild canine that was thriving and increasing its range. Coyotes and red wolves mated and produced hybrid offspring with the characteristics of both. In the early 1970s the red wolf was fast disappearing as a pure genetic entity. As one biologist put it, "They were simply mating themselves into oblivion."

The red wolf *is* a distinct species, with behavior and physical features, including body and bone measurements, that distinguish it from coyotes and gray wolves. The Fish and Wildlife Service launched a recovery plan for the species in 1972. It called for creating a buffer zone between coyote and wolf populations. This plan didn't work. Crossbreeding with coyotes continued, and biologists decided that the red wolf could not be saved in the wild with coyotes around. Perhaps life in captivity would save the species.

By 1980 there were no more red wolves in the wild. Four hundred animals had been trapped. They were all examined closely; sometimes X-rays were taken of their skulls. Most turned out to be coyotes or coyote-wolf hybrids. Forty animals were judged to be pure red wolf and were taken to Tacoma, Washington, where a captive breeding colony was set up at the Point Defiance Zoo. The wolves were soon moved 40 miles from Tacoma and kept in large pens with plenty of natural vegetation and little human contact. From the start, biologist Curtis Carley of the Fish and Wildlife Service wanted conditions kept as wild as possible. He said, "We were quite concerned about keeping the red wolf a wild animal and not making it merely a zoo one."

By crossbreeding certain animals and studying their young, biologists were able to weed out some that were not true red wolves. Some pure red wolves or their offspring were transferred to other zoos in order to avoid loss of the whole species to an outbreak of disease. While the numbers of captive wolves grew to about seventy-five, the Fish and Wildlife Service scouted for sites where the species could be reintroduced.

One possibility, proposed in 1981, was an area called the Land Between the Lakes, in Kentucky and Tennessee. But opposition from hunters and farmers was strong. An environmental group, Defenders of Wildlife, also opposed release of red wolves there. Coyotes were present, and chances of success seemed slim.

Another, better site soon turned up—one that had no coyotes within several hundred miles. An insurance company donated to the Fish and Wildlife Service 118,000 acres of wooded peninsula on the North Carolina coast. In 1984 it became the Alligator River National Wildlife Refuge, to which about 20,000 additional acres have since been added. And in 1986, eight red wolves arrived at the refuge by helicopter. The wolves weren't let go immediately. This is called a "hard" release. Instead, they experienced a "soft" release.

For six months they were kept in large, isolated pens. At first they were fed dog food, then road-killed wildlife, and during the final month, live prey. They were left alone for long periods and became increasingly wary of humans. In May 1987 the pen doors were left open and the wolves were on their own. For the first time, a native species that no longer existed in the wild had been returned from a captive breeding population to its natural habitat.

Three wolves died in less than a year: two of natural causes, one

From a totally captive population, the red wolf has been returned to two wild areas in the Southeast.

hit by an automobile. Such losses were expected. The first year also brought extraordinary news: two families had produced litters of cubs.

The Fish and Wildlife Service brought more adult red wolves to the refuge in 1987 and let them go in 1988. Through such releases and natural reproduction, biologists hope that wolf numbers will reach twenty-five to thirty-five in the early 1990s. They also expect the wolves to spread to nearby habitats.

In 1989 a pair of red wolves were released to a wilderness area on Horn Island, in the Gulf of Mexico off the Mississippi coast. Red wolves will eventually be released in at least one other mainland site in the Southeast. The species will probably never exist in great numbers in the wild, but human intervention has given it a chance to persist on its own again.

Do Ferrets and Condors Have a Future?

Promising results with the red wolf raised hopes about other possibilities, for example, release of captive-born Mexican wolves in the Southwest and panthers in Florida. Success for the red wolf seemed especially important for the condors and ferrets that were removed completely from the wild during the late 1980s. However, each species had its unique history, needs, and relations with other organisms—including humans—that could either raise or dash hopes for its return to the wild.

Black-footed ferrets live in prairie dog burrows and feed primarily on these rodents. As ranchers waged war on prairie dogs, ferret numbers dropped. They were eliminated from most of their western range, which had stretched from Canada to Mexico and from the Great Plains to the Rockies. A few survived in northern states, and in 1971 the Fish and Wildlife Service caught six in South Dakota and attempted to breed them in captivity. The project failed when the last captive ferret died in 1978. By 1980 many people thought the black-footed ferret was extinct.

Some biologists investigated reports of sightings and searched prairie dog colonies for signs of ferrets. However, it was a Wyoming ranch dog named Shep that collected a ferret in 1981, when he killed a male near his food bowl one night. This event led to the discovery of a ferret colony in northwestern Wyoming, near the town of Meeteetse. By the spring of 1982, biologists had counted at least thirty ferrets at Meeteetse.

Between 1981 and 1988, the fortunes of the ferrets rose, fell, and rose again. The feelings of wildlife biologists went on the same roller coaster. Hopes rose as the ferret population grew to 128 by the summer of 1984. (Their numbers were counted at night by shining high-intensity lights over different areas of the 8,000-acre prairie dog town and spotting the reflections of ferret eyes.) There was talk but no action about removing some of the colony in order to start a second population.

Ferret numbers plummeted in 1985. A disease called plague was blamed at first, and several tons of insecticide were applied to thousands of prairie dog burrows in an attempt to kill plague-carrying fleas. Fearing that all the ferrets might die, the Wyoming Fish and Game Department captured all it could find at Meeteetse, just six. These began to sicken and die of a disease called canine distemper— apparently the real cause of the population's collapse.

For a few weeks it seemed that the species was gone. But six more ferrets were captured, proved to be free of distemper, and were vaccinated against it. On them, it seemed, rested the fate of the species. At a laboratory near Laramie, biologists of the Fish and Game Department tried to raise and breed black-footed ferrets in captivity.

Several additional wild ferrets were caught at Meeteetse and added to the captive colony. They thrived on a diet of cat food, hamsters, and prairie dogs. Two females produced litters of young in 1987, and thirteen females produced 34 kits that survived in 1988. The colony was growing, and biologists began to plan the reintroduction of ferrets to wild habitat.

In the summer of 1988, small captive prairie dog towns were set up near the breeding laboratory. Dr. Tom Thorne, manager of the breeding program, said, "Since no one has reintroduced ferrets before, we don't know how important this is going to be . . . . But you can't take a captive animal and just dump him out and expect him to get along. He's got to know how to survive in a burrow system, how to kill prairie dogs, how to dig them out when they plug themselves in. You can't teach them that in a hard-floor cage."

Attempts to release some ferrets in the wild will not begin until the captive colony numbers at least 250. The first reintroduction could occur in 1991. Since a single ferret roams over a hundred acres, a large area with a complex of several prairie dog colonies will be needed to sustain a population of 100 to 200 ferrets.

Biologists hope to find ten or more sites, each with at least 7,000 acres of land. Some exist on the vast public lands of the West, but some especially desirable areas may be on private ranches. It remains to be seen whether landowners can be induced to tolerate large prairie dog

In the mid-1980s, a disease outbreak nearly wiped out the last black-footed ferrets in existence.

colonies on their grazing lands. Restoring thriving populations of the black-footed ferret in several states is possible but will cost an estimated $1.5 million a year for many years to come.

Plans to reintroduce captive-born California condors are more complex and perhaps more expensive. In 1988 no condors existed in the wild. Twenty-eight lived at two zoos, and only one of these had been born in captivity. Nevertheless, biologists at the Fish and Wildlife Service's Condor Research Center in Ventura were cautiously optimistic.

The condor is a red-headed vulture that weighs about twenty pounds and has a wingspan of nine or more feet—the longest in North America. In the late Pleistocene, more than 10,000 years ago, these birds were probably abundant and widespread in the West. Their fossils have also been found in Florida. Carrion-eaters, condors had plentiful food in those days, when North America was the habitat of early horses, camels, mammoths, bison, ground sloths, saber-toothed

By successfully reproducing in captivity, the black-footed ferret has a chance of being reestablished in the wild.

cats, and other large mammals. Fossil evidence from cliff caves where condors nested indicates that the birds fed on the carcasses of these creatures. However, many of these mammals became extinct at the end of the Pleistocene. Then the numbers and range of California condors began to shrink.

They survived near the Pacific Coast, perhaps by feeding mostly on beached carcasses of whales, seals, and other marine animals. When settlers brought cattle and other livestock to the West, condors had a new food supply and expanded their range inland. They were seen in Utah and Arizona during the late 1800s. Livestock carcasses continued to be their primary food, right up until 1987, when the last wild condors were captured and placed in captive breeding colonies.

We still do not understand all of the reasons for the modern decline of this species. We do know that some were shot, that food was sometimes contaminated, and that land developers reduced condor habitats, including vital food-foraging areas. The condor also has a low reproductive rate. It doesn't mate until six or seven years of age, and then females usually produce just one egg every two years.

Efforts to save to condor began in the late 1930s. Many millions of dollars have been spent by the Fish and Wildlife Service, the state of California, and the National Audubon Society in a collective effort to reverse the condor's decline. Not that the researchers always agree on the best strategy. Far from it. In 1985, after six wild birds had died in just a few months, the California Department of Fish and Game urged that the last few wild birds be put in captivity. At first this was vigorously opposed by the Fish and Wildlife Service and the National Audubon Society. Among the concerns was that removing all birds from the wild would reduce chances of protecting the condor's habitat from developers.

The condor's main nesting and roosting sites are on public lands, in three national forests. But most of its food-foraging habitat is on private land. One key foraging area of 13,600 acres was acquired in 1987 and became the Bitter Creek National Wildlife Refuge.

In 1988 and 1989 the birth of several condor chicks in captivity raised hopes for the eventual return of birds to the wild. Several birds reached sexual maturity in the late 1980s and were expected to begin producing young. In order to speed up condor reproduction, researchers plan to use a simple but effective trick that has increased the numbers of peregrine falcons raised in captivity. If a condor's egg is "stolen" soon after it is laid, the bird responds by producing another egg. In this way a bird can be induced to lay two or three eggs a year, rather than one. All of the eggs can be incubated and produce young. This is called double- or triple-clutching. Application of this technique may increase condors sufficiently to allow release of some birds in the wild by the mid-1990s.

Researchers are devoting plenty of attention to the needs of condors should a wild population in fact be established. They are concerned about how young birds will learn to fly and soar, find food, and compete with other scavengers. To learn about this, in early 1989 biologists released some young Andean condors that were donated by

If California condors reproduce well in captivity, young birds could be released outdoors by the mid-1990s.

zoos. After two or three years of study, these surrogate condors will be captured and released in South America.

Biologists expect that feeding sites may have to be set up in the California condor's foraging areas in order to provide the birds with uncontaminated food. A plentiful supply of livestock carcasses may eventually allow a greater than normal number of condors to live in their 50,000-square-mile range.

Choices and Challenges

The spectacle of wild condors soaring freely over the land is eagerly anticipated by many. But this is not a unanimous feeling: some wonder why we don't "pull the plug" on the condor since it was a species in decline even before European settlers came to North America. Few scientists share this view, but they do worry about the choices that must be made in allocating limited funds for saving wildlife. Consider this: the sum spent annually on condors and black-footed ferrets is more than that for all endangered reptiles, invertebrates, and plants put together.

Dr. Tom Cade of the Peregrine Fund said, "Reintroductions are last-ditch and desperate efforts . . . they can work, but they take lots of time and lots of money." (His efforts have been unusually successful, with nearly 2,500 captive-reared falcons released to the wild since 1975.)

Furthermore, as more of the natural world is cut down, plowed up, or paved over, the number of species in need of help—perhaps a costly captive breeding program—will increase. There is danger in putting too much emphasis on single prominent species and thereby diverting attention and money from the task of saving habitat. To this argument some ecologists respond: "When you save one species, everything that it needs to survive goes along with it." For example, saving black-footed ferrets also saves prairie dogs and the burrowing owls, snakes, insects, and other invertebrates that are part of a prairie dog colony ecosystem.

In fact, habitat is often saved as a direct result of a captive breeding and reintroduction program. For example, masked bobwhite quail had died out in Arizona and nearly so in Mexico. They were bred successfully in captivity. Then 118,000 acres in southern Arizona became their new home and also a new reserve—the Buenos Aires National Wildlife Refuge. Many kinds of wild animals and plants will benefit from establishment of the refuge.

In defense of captive breeding, Roger Birkel, general curator at the St. Louis Zoo, said, "The first priority should be the wild, but some species are on such a precipitous decline that we need to get captive breeding programs going for them now before it is too late."

Zoos have a rather spotty record in wildlife conservation. To attract the public, they have always focused attention on "charismatic megavertebrates"—appealing large animals, mostly mammals and birds. Historically, zoos cared mostly about the welfare of the individual animals in their collections, with less concern about the

Burrowing owls, snakes, and other species benefit when a prairie dog colony is given protection.

51

well-being of wild populations. This attitude is not entirely dead. In 1988, a controversy erupted over zoos in the United States borrowing giant pandas from China for temporary displays.

As a result of poaching and loss of habitat, fewer than 1,000 pandas survive in the wild. Those in captivity have not reproduced well, though biologists are working on ways to improve on this record. Pandas are tremendously popular and give zoos an opportunity to make people aware of the threats to the survival of pandas and of all endangered species. But pandas also give a huge boost to a zoo's revenues and membership.

This "panda profiteering" was criticized by the World Wildlife Fund because some pandas loaned by China were of breeding age. The plight of the species makes any missed opportunity for reproduction a terrible loss. In 1988 the American Association of Zoological Parks and Aquariums belatedly adopted a strict policy against importing pandas capable of breeding. The policy also requires that money earned from temporary panda exhibits be used only for saving the species.

Most zoos in the United States and other wealthy nations have made sweeping changes in efforts to save world wildlife. Zoos and aquariums are growing in size and trying to display animals in more natural-looking surroundings. They try to foster normal behavior, including reproduction. Some have set up research centers, particularly to learn how to successfully breed wild animals in captivity. A lot has been learned, and zoos seldom need to take an animal from the wild. In 1989, 90 percent of the new mammals and 75 percent of the new birds in captivity were zoo-born.

Knowledge gained at United States zoos has sometimes proved useful in captive breeding of endangered species. Zoo experience with the abundant Andean condor, for example, helped biologists plan the breeding program for the highly endangered California condor. Zoo biologists have also adopted and developed techniques from livestock breeding, such as freezing sperm, eggs, and embryos for future use.

They have used hormones to stimulate production of eggs in a female Eld's deer (a rare South Asian species), then fertilized the eggs, removed the embryos, and implanted them in females of abundant white-tailed deer. This quickly increased the numbers of Eld's deer.

Zoo biologists share information with other zoos because they recognize that animal populations have to be managed *across* zoos, taking the entire captive population into account. All individuals of a species represent a "pool" of genetic characteristics. Keeping the gene pool as diverse as possible is vital for a species' survival. For example, the genes that convey resistance to certain diseases are often present in the eggs or sperm of only a few animals in a population. If those animals fail to reproduce and die, the population loses that disease resistance. Increasingly, zoos plan the breeding of their captive animals so that genetic diversity is maintained.

As the 1988 controversy over pandas showed, people in the United States cannot ignore the effect of their actions on wildlife all over the earth. Our care of captive species in zoos, the raw materials we import from abroad, the pesticides we export—all have an impact on the world's wildlife. We do great harm, but our political and financial support of international animal and plant conservation also does great good.

This book has concentrated on wildlife of North America, but concern about wildlife cannot stop at a nation's or continent's borders. We now know that 100 million monarch butterflies from the eastern United States and Canada fly to central Mexico every year and concentrate there in a few patches of forest. Loss of that habitat might doom the butterflies. We also know that destruction of tropical rain forests in Latin America is reducing the numbers of certain songbirds that summer in the United States and Canada. Saving habitat here does not ensure survival of the birds. We must also save habitat there.

Wildlife need not perish if we keep working, at home and abroad.

Saving Nongame Wildlife

Most wildlife species are nongame—animals that are not hunted or fished for. After decades of emphasis on game animals, many states now have programs aimed at protecting nongame. Often the first step is research to learn about the status of wildlife species and their habitats. Then action can be taken to acquire, protect, and manage the habitats. Many states also produce posters, booklets, and films in an effort to educate the public about the value of nongame wildlife. The following list is a sampling of nongame projects funded by five states:

Colorado
* River otters are an endangered species in Colorado. More than 100 otters have been obtained from other states and released in remote waterways around the state.
* In the early 1970s no peregrine falcons bred successfully in Colorado. After more than a dozen years of releasing young peregrines in suitable habitats, 23 pairs of peregrine falcons produced young in 1987.
* Colorado biologists have found populations of the mountain wood frog, a species threatened with extinction, and have made efforts to influence land and water use practices in order to protect their habitats.

New York

• The common tern, least tern, roseate tern, and piping plover are colony-nesting waterbirds threatened with extinction in New York State. Action has been taken to maintain and protect their nesting habitats.

• To communicate the value of wildlife to young people, state biologists conduct workshops for teachers. Educational packets have been distributed to 10,000 teachers in the upper elementary grades. And several thousand members of 4-H Clubs have been involved in creating new wildlife refuges within their communities.

Texas

• Surveys have been conducted in order to determine the numbers and distribution of wildcats, including the ocelot and jaguarundi. Similar studies were planned in 1988–1989 for Texas kangaroo rats, prairie dogs, and diamondback terrapins.

Wildlife biologists have helped peregrine falcons return to their former range in Colorado.

- A study of the red-cockaded woodpecker, an endangered species, showed that its numbers had dropped sharply in Texas. Most of its favored habitat—open forest of old pine trees—has been cut down. Biologists recommended that private landowners be given incentives to protect the remaining habitat of this species.

Virginia

- Wildlife biologists have searched for caves in order to learn about the status of three endangered species—the gray, big-eared, and Indiana bats. Steps are being taken to protect caves and to encourage cave explorers to leave bats alone.
- Research has given biologists a picture of the status of many nongame species in Virginia, including barn owls, flying squirrels, great blue herons, and fox squirrels. Two fish species—the orangefin madtom and the Roanoke logperch—were discovered to be more widespread than previously thought.
- Among the educational materials produced by the Virginia Department of Game and Inland Fisheries is a folder ("Wildlife Plantings, Boxes, and Platforms") that tells how to make bird houses, bird feeders, bird-nesting platforms, and even bat houses.

Wisconsin

- No barn owls were known to nest in Wisconsin during the early 1980s. A captive breeding program was begun, and 22 barn owls were released in 1987. Nesting boxes are being placed on interior walls of barns and silos for the owls.
- Natural areas must sometimes be managed in order to maintain desirable wildlife habitats. The work includes controlled burning of prairies and pulling purple loosestrife (an aggressive alien weed) from lakes and ponds. Volunteers helped with this work, as they do with many projects in Wisconsin and other states. Write to your state's natural resources or fish and game department for information about its nongame programs.

In Wisconsin, the barn owl is another nongame species that is being reestablished in the wild.

Working to Save Wildlife

In North America there are countless opportunities for young people to help wild animals (and plants) on a volunteer basis. The effort can range from simple membership in a national wildlife organization to actual work that has a direct effect on local wildlife. It can include caring for injured birds and mammals (saving a few individuals), as well as political lobbying for the protection of vital habitats (saving entire populations).

Community nature centers welcome help with a variety of projects, as do some town, city, county, or state parks. Also inquire about such local youth groups as the Boy Scouts, Girl Scouts, and 4-H Clubs, which in some areas are active in wildlife conservation. Contact the federal Fish and Wildlife Service to learn about nearby refuges. It operates such areas in every state except West Virginia; many of these refuges have opportunities for volunteers. Help is also needed for the agency's Endangered Species Program. For information, write to: United States Fish and Wildlife Service, Department of the Interior, 18th and C Streets, NW, Washington, D.C. 20240.

Listed below are several national organizations that also encourage citizen involvement in wildlife projects. The most complete listing of wildlife conservation groups, on both the federal and state level, can be found in *The Conservation Directory*, published annually by the National Wildlife Federation (address below). In addition, the quarterly magazine *Buzzworm: The Environmental Journal* publishes several pages of volunteer and job opportunities in each issue (address: 1818 16th Street, Boulder, Colorado, 80302).

Defenders of Wildlife aims to "preserve, enhance, and protect the natural abundance and diversity of wildlife." For information about membership and its activist network, write to: Defenders of Wildlife, 1244 19th Street, NW, Washington, D.C. 20036.

Earthwatch enlists the help of enthusiastic amateurs in scientific projects around the world. Volunteers pay for the opportunity to work on archeological digs and other research projects, including studies of wildlife habitats and endangered species. For information, write to: Earthwatch, 680 Mount Auburn Street, P.O. Box 403, Watertown, Massachusetts 02272.

Greenpeace is particularly concerned with preserving marine ecosystems. In Florida its members patrol ocean beaches in order to locate and protect sea turtle nests. For information about this and other programs, write to: Greenpeace, Public Information, 1436 U Street, NW, Washington, D.C. 20009.

The *National Audubon Society* is one of the nation's foremost wildlife conservation groups. In addition to more than 500 local chapters, its "Audubon Activist Network" is made up of citizens who want to take direct action in efforts to save habitats and protect threatened species. For information, write to: National Audubon Society, 950 Third Avenue, New York, N.Y. 10022.

The *National Wildlife Federation* has affiliates in each state that are made up mostly of "sportsmen's" (hunting and fishing) groups. Many have programs aimed at aiding wildlife populations. For information about these and about the work of the national organization, write to: National Wildlife Federation, 1412 16th Street, NW, Washington, D.C. 20036.

The Nature Conservancy's mission is "to find, protect, and maintain the best examples of communities, ecosystems, and endangered species in the world." It owns and manages about 1,000 preserves, where volunteer workers are often needed. For information, write to: The Nature Conservancy, 1815 North Lynn Street, Arlington, Virginia 22209.

The *Student Conservation Association* enlists the help of conservation-minded students (ages 16 to 18) who want to work and learn during their summer vacations. For information, write to: The Student Conservation Association, P.O. Box 550, Charlestown, New Hampshire 03603.

A volunteer of the Student Conservation Association assists in an elk study at Yellowstone National Park.

Further Reading

Banks, Vic. "The Red Wolf Gets a Second Chance to Live by Its Wits." *Smithsonian,* March 1988, pp. 100–107.

Booth, William. "Reintroducing a Political Animal." *Science,* July 8, 1988, pp. 154–158.

Cohn, Jeffrey. "Captive Breeding for Conservation." *Bioscience,* May 1988, pp. 312–316.

Cohn, Jeffrey. "Red Wolf in the Wilderness." *Bioscience,* May 1987, pp. 313–316.

Dunlap, Thomas. *Saving America's Wildlife.* Princeton, New Jersey: Princeton University Press, 1988.

Ehrlich, Paul and Anne. *Extinction: The Causes and Consequences of the Disappearance of Species.* New York: Random House, 1981.

Grove, Noel. "Quietly Conserving Nature." *National Geographic,* December 1988, pp. 818–845.

Kennedy, David. "What's New at the Zoo?" *Technology Review,* April 1987, pp. 67–73.

Lawren, Bill. "The High Cost of Neglecting Wildlife." *National Wildlife,* April-May, 1989, pp. 4–8.

Newmark, William. "A Land-bridge Island Perspective on Mammalian Extinctions in Western North American Parks." *Nature,* January 29, 1987, pp. 430–432.

Norton, Bryan, editor. *The Preservation of Species.* Princeton, New Jersey: Princeton University Press, 1986.

Patent, Dorothy Hinshaw. *The Whooping Crane: A Comeback Story.* New York: Clarion, 1988.

Peters, Robert, and Joan Darling. "The Greenhouse Effect and Nature Reserves." *Bioscience,* December 1985, pp. 707–717.

Pringle, Laurence, *Restoring Our Earth.* Hillside, New Jersey: Enslow Publishers, 1987.

Pringle, Laurence. *What Shall We Do With the Land?: Choices for America.* New York: T. Y. Crowell, 1981.

Roberts, Leslie. "Conservationists in Panda-monium." *Science,* July 29, 1988, pp. 529–531.

Simberloff, Daniel. "What a Species Needs to Survive." *The Nature Conservancy News,* November-December 1983, pp. 18–22.

Schwartz, Anne. "Bright Future for a Desert Refugium." *Nature Conservancy News,* September-October 1984, pp. 13–17.

Steinhart, Peter. "A Wolf in the Eye." *Audubon,* January 1988, pp. 78–89.

Thorne, Tom, and Elizabeth Williams. "Disease and Endangered Species: The Black-footed Ferret as a Recent Example." *Conservation Biology,* March 1988, pp. 66–74.

Trefethen, James. *An American Crusade for Wildlife.* New York: Winchester Press, 1975.

Wilkinson, Todd. "Yellowstone's Poaching War." *Defenders,* May-June 1988, pp. 30–36.

Williams, Ted. "Resurrection of the Wild Turkey." *Audubon,* January 1984, pp. 71–75.

Index

A

acid rain, 7-8
Alaska, 13, 29, 34, 36
alien species, 21, 31, 33, 56
Alligator River National Wildlife
    Refuge, 42, 44
animal-plant communities, 10-11, 33,
    50-51
Aransas National Wildlife Refuge, 31
Arizona, 48, 51
Ash Meadows National Wildlife
    Refuge, 17-18, 33

B

bats, 56
bears, 24
beavers, 27, 29-30, 39
birds, 7, 14, 15, 20, 21, 23, 33, 51,
    53. *See also* specific
    species.
Birkel, Roger, 51
bison, 27, 39, 40, 47
Bitter Creek National Wildlife Refuge,
    48
blackbirds, 7
Bosque del Apache National Wildlife
    Refuge, 31
Buenos Aires National Wildlife
    Refuge, 51
butterflies, 5, 18, 53

C

Cade, Tom, 50
California, 5, 14, 16, 21-22, 27,
    34-35, 36, 48
Canada, 13, 30, 31, 34, 36, 37, 38,
    39, 44, 53
captive breeding, 5, 40-51, 52-55, 56
Carley, Curtis, 42
CITES treaty, 24, 26
Colorado, 16, 19, 36, 54
condors, 5, 7, 40, 44, 47-50, 52
Congress, U.S., 7, 14, 37
Connecticut, 16
Crane Reservation & Wildlife Refuge,
    18-19
cranes, whooping, 31, 33
crows, 12
coyotes, 33, 37, 41, 42

D

deer, 18-19, 24, 39, 53
Defenders of Wildlife, 37, 42
Diamond, Jared, 20
diversity, 5, 14, 33, 53
ducks, 7-8, 12, 14, 22, 27

E

eagles, 8, 12, 24
egrets, 27
Eisner, Thomas, 27
elk, 19-20, 27, 39
endangered species, 16, 17, 24, 27,
    31, 34, 36, 41, 52, 54,
    56, 58, 59
environmental groups, 14, 18, 42. *See
    also* specific groups.
Everglades National Park, 11, 21
extinction, 5, 9, 26, 40, 44

F

falcons, peregrine, 49, 54
federal wildlife refuges, 12-13, 14, 15,
    21, 30, 58. *See also*
    specific refuges.
ferrets, black-footed, 7, 40, 44-47, 50
fire, as natural force, 9, 18, 56
Fish and Wildlife Service, 18, 22-23,
    31, 33, 36, 41, 42, 44,
    47, 48, 58
fish and fishing, 12, 14, 15, 22, 27,
    54, 56
fisher, 33-34
Florida, 11, 21, 31, 33, 44, 47
foxes, 12
frogs, 54

G

game animals, 12, 14, 33
geese, 14
Georgia, 33
Glacier National Park, 36, 37, 38
Grays Lake National Wildlife Refuge, 31

H

habitat needs of different species, 9,
    11, 18, 20-21, 48, 53
habitat preservation, 5, 12-14, 16,
    20-21, 27, 50, 53
hawks, 12
heath hen, 9-10
hunters and hunting, 9, 12, 14, 15,
    19, 29, 33, 42, 54

I

Idaho, 31, 34, 36, 37, 38
Illinois, 31, 33
insects, 7, 8, 10-11, 20, 50
Isle Royale National Park, 36
Izaak Walton League, 14

K

Kentucky, 42
Kesterson National Wildlife Refuge,
    21-22
kite, snail, 7-8

L

loons, common 7-8
Louisiana, 41
M
Maine, 30
manatees, 7
Martha's Vineyard, 9-10
Massachusetts, 9-10, 18-19
Mech, L. David, 39
Mexico, 44, 51, 53
Michigan, 8-9, 30-31, 36
Minnesota, 31, 36, 37, 39
Mississippi, 44
Missouri, 30
Montana, 30, 34, 36, 37
moose, 39
N
National Audubon Society, 14, 24, 31, 48
national forests, 13, 14, 36, 48
national parks, 13, 14, 20, 21, 23-24, 39. *See also* specific parks.
National Park Service, 17
National Wildlife Federation, 14
Nature Conservancy, 16-18
Nevada, 17-18, 21, 33
New Mexico, 31
New York, 5, 9, 16, 18, 29, 33, 36, 55
New York Zoological Park, 40
nongame animals, 14-16, 54-56
North Carolina, 5, 42
O
oil spills, 34
Oklahoma, 14, 40
opossums, 8
Oregon, 34, 36
oryx, Arabian, 40
ospreys, 8, 24
otters, river, 34, 54
otters, sea, 27, 34-35
owls, 24, 33, 50, 56
P
pandas, giant, 52, 53
pelicans, 8, 12
Pennsylvania, 12
Peregrine Fund, 50
pesticides, 8, 21, 53
Point Defiance Zoo, 41
population size as a factor in wildlife survival, 9-10, 20, 45, 53
prairie dogs, 44, 45-47, 50, 55
prairie restoration, 33
President's Commission on Americans Outdoors, 21
pronghorns, 27, 39
pupfish, Devil's Hole, 17

Q

quail, masked bobwhite, 51
R
raccoons, 8
Red Rock Lakes Migratory Bird Refuge, 30
reintroduction of wildlife, 27-39, 45-47, 50
Rocky Mountain National Park, 19-20, 23-24
Rocky Mountains, 30, 36
Roosevelt, President Theodore, 12
S
sheep, bighorn, 23-24
snails, apple, 11
South Dakota, 44
spoonbills, 12
Stillwater Wildlife Management Area, 21
swans, trumpeter, 27, 30-31, 33
T
Tall Grass Prairie National Preserve, 14
tax checkoffs for nongame, 16
Tennessee, 42
terns, 55
Texas, 31, 41, 55-56
Thompson, James 24
Thorne, Tom, 46
Trout Unlimited, 14
turkeys, wild, 27, 29
Turnage, William, 39
turtles, snapping, 31
U
Utah, 48
V
Virginia, 56
W
warbler, Kirtland's, 8-9, 18
Washington, 36, 41-42
water pollution, 21-23
wildcats, 55
Wilderness Society, 39
wildlife, value of, 5, 7
Wisconsin, 20, 30, 34, 36, 56
World Wildlife Fund, 52
wolves, gray, 19, 35-39, 41
wolves, red, 5, 40-44
woodpecker, red-cockaded, 56
Wyoming, 45-46
Y
Yellowstone National Park, 30, 36, 37, 38-39
Z
zoos, 31, 40, 47, 50, 51-53